Discover India
State by State

OFF TO HARYANA

SONIA MEHTA

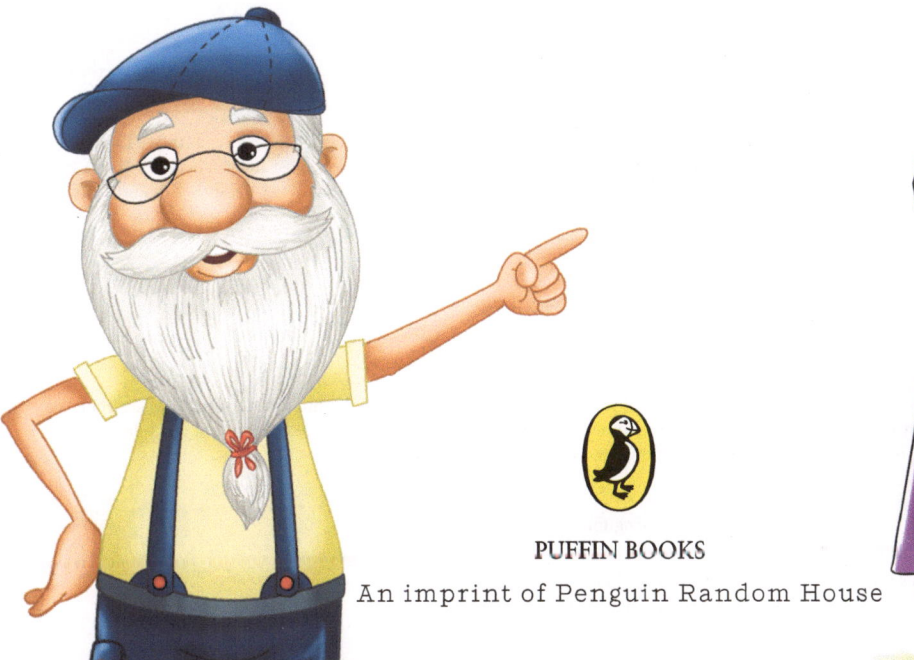

PUFFIN BOOKS
An imprint of Penguin Random House

PUFFIN BOOKS

USA | Canada | UK | Ireland | Australia | New Zealand | India | South Africa | China | Singapore

Puffin Books is part of the Penguin Random House group of companies whose addresses can be found at global.penguinrandomhouse.com

Published by Penguin Random House India Pvt. Ltd
4th Floor, Capital Tower 1, MG Road,
Gurugram 122 002, Haryana, India

Penguin
Random House
India

First published in Puffin Books by Penguin Random House India 2018

Text, design and illustrations copyright © Quadrum Solutions Pvt. Ltd 2018
Series copyright © Penguin Random House India 2018

Picture Credits

ISBN 9780143440895

Design and layout by Quadrum Solutions Pvt. Ltd

Printed at Repro India Limited

www.penguin.co.in

This is a legitimate digitally printed version of the book and therefore might not
have certain extra finishing on the cover.

Hello Kids!

I'm so happy you are reading this book. India is an incredible country and there are lots of things about it that we never get to hear about.

I discovered India because my father was in the Indian army. He was posted to many places all over India—and we dutifully followed him. Can you imagine that by the time I was in the tenth standard, I had changed nine schools? Of course it was hard making new friends almost every year, but the good part was that I got to live in so many places. Right from Kerala, where I was born, to Kashmir, Jhansi, Shillong, Chandigarh, Goa . . . the list is long.

Every time I go to a new place, I feel amazed at how different each state is from the other—and yet, how similar. Did you know that we can see monuments from the Stone Age right here in India? Or that we have more than twenty official languages, and most Indians know three or four on an average? Or even that some of the world's most amazing scientific marvels were invented in India?

Oh, there are many, many, many fun and fantastic things about the states of India, which we simply must get to know.

So get your backpack ready, get set to meet some new friends and join me on a fun trip as we **DISCOVER INDIA, STATE BY STATE**.

I hope you enjoy reading this book as much as I have enjoyed writing it. I would love to hear from you. So do write to me at sonia.mehta@quadrumltd.com.

Lots of love,

Sonia Aunty

Mishki and Pushka have come to visit Earth from their home planet, Zoomba. They have never seen such an amazing place. Zoomba doesn't have trees and mountains and rivers like Earth does. But the people look exactly the same. When they come to Earth, they meet a sweet old man whom they call Daadu Dolma. Daadu Dolma shows them all the wonderful places in India and tells Mishki and Pushka all about them.

Mishki and Pushka can't believe what they see. They have seen a lot of Earth, but they have never, ever seen a place like India.

They are off to explore India state by state :)

Mishki

Mishki is a curious little girl. She is always asking loads of questions. On her home planet, she is always getting into trouble for poking her nose into things that are not her business.

Pushka

Pushka is Mishki's brother. He loves adventure. He is always ready to try a new challenge. Whether it's climbing a mountain, or diving into a cold, cold sea, he is up for it.

Daadu Dolma

Daadu Dolma is a wise old man who has lived on Earth longer than the mountains and seas. No one knows quite how old he is, but he certainly has been around. He knows everything about everything.

Mishki and Pushka are very curious because they don't know much about the state they are about to visit.

'Daadu, what should we expect to see in Haryana? What is it famous for?' Pushka asks, looking excited.

'Well, you could say that Haryana is where a lot of India's history was born. Some of the greatest events in Indian history occurred here,' explains Daadu.

'That's super!' exclaims Mishki, clapping her hands. She loves history. 'I shall take my camera along and take lots of pictures.'

'Yes,' agrees Daadu, 'there is a lot to see in Haryana, so you had better be packed and ready.'

Mishki and Pushka quickly pack their bags. They can't wait to leave. They are

OFF TO HARYANA!!!

A SNEAK PEEK

NEIGHBOURS ALL AROUND

For such a small state, Haryana certainly has a lot of neighbours. Punjab, Himachal Pradesh, Uttarakhand, Uttar Pradesh, Delhi and Rajasthan surround it. Wow! Things sure must be busy around here.

ON THE MAP

To see exactly where Haryana is on the map of India, go to

http://www.mapsofindia.com/maps/india/india-political-map.htm

THE GEOGRAPHIC TWOSOME

There are two main geographic regions in Haryana—one is a vast, flat, fertile plain; the other is a small strip of hilly land in the form of a part of the Shivalik Range. Most of the land here is wonderful for farming.

Haryana means 'the home of God'— hari (God) and ayana (home).

SHARING A CAPITAL

Haryana shares its capital city with its neighbour Punjab. The city of Chandigarh, which lies within the Chandigarh Union Territory, is the capital of both Punjab and Haryana. This is because Punjab and Haryana were, at one time, a large common state. Why were they divided? We'll find out soon.

RIVER FACT

Haryana has one main river that waters it—the famous Yamuna. The Yamuna has water all through the year, which means that it is perennial. There are smaller seasonal streams that wander through the state, after gushing down the Shivalik Range. The Ghaggar is the most important of these.

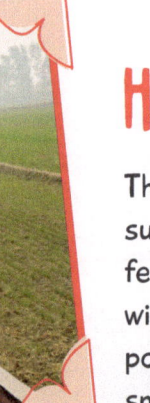

HOT AND COLD

This state has an extreme climate. This means that summers are very hot and dry, and will leave you feeling like a potato baking in an oven. But during winters, the temperature can drop below freezing point—cold enough to make ice cream. It doesn't snow here though.

SOME MORE TREES, PLEASE!

Haryana has no major forests. Eucalyptus trees have been planted along the highways and wastelands. Shisham trees also grow near the canals. But other than these, there are only shrubs and small trees that sprout here and there.

The Yamuna is considered to be one of India's most holy rivers.

RAIN, RAIN, COME AGAIN

Even though most of Haryana is great for farming, the rain does not help it too much. The state does not have a heavy monsoon, and some parts of it often face drought. The farmers have to depend more on canals and wells for irrigation. Ironically, the areas near the Yamuna sometimes have heavy floods. It's an extreme situation, all right.

TREE PATTERN

Mishki has decided to plant trees in a pattern. Can you draw the tree that comes next in each row?

FIELDS AND FARMS

There are many, many fields and farms across Haryana. Much of the rice and wheat we eat in India is produced here. That's not all. The farmers also grow vast quantities of cotton, sugarcane, corn, millet, potatoes and lots more. Farmers stay busy in this state.

Pearl millet fields look lovely in the sun.

The people here love their rotis because of the wonderful wheat grown here.

COWS AND BUFFALOES

The dairy business is big here too, with many farmers breeding cows, buffaloes and bullocks for dairy as well as to plough the land.

WILD AND WONDERFUL

There are some large species, like leopards, jackals and wild boars, that roam the few forests Haryana has. Colourful birds, like parakeets, sunbirds, buntings, bulbuls and kingfishers, flit around. On the ground, you will see plenty of smaller mammals, like squirrels, bats and gerbils.

FUN FACTS

State animal
Blackbuck

State tree
Peepal

State bird
Black francolin

State flower
Lotus

Time to draw

Mishki loves to draw. She has drawn a parakeet that she saw in Haryana. Can you draw a similar one?

Draw here

CITY CITY BANG BANG

Haryana has some big and very important cities—both historical and modern. Let's visit a few.

GURUGRAM
(EARLIER GURGAON)

This city is part of the National Capital Region (NCR) of India and is located very close to New Delhi. It has become a very important industrial and financial hub, and it's considered to be one of the most modern cities in India.

FARIDABAD

This is one of Haryana's largest cities. Also in the National Capital Region of India, it is a very important industrial centre. Faridabad is home to the Surajkund Mela that showcases the vibrant handicrafts of India.

Guru Jambheshwar University of Science and Technology, Hisar

HISAR

This city was ruled by some of India's greatest dynasties, like the Mauryan dynasty. Now it is a modern city with factories and educational institutions.

I want to visit all these cities!

ROHTAK

Here is a city with incredible history. Many Indian and international companies have their factories here.

Tilyar Lake, Rohtak

Kabuli Bagh Mosque, Panipat

PANIPAT

Many fearsome battles were fought here. Now, it is a peaceful city and is also called the City of Weavers, as it is an important textile hub.

HIDDEN WORDS

How many smaller words can you make from the word FARIDABAD? Mishki has made one to start you off.

FARIDABAD

FAR _____   _____   _____

_____   _____   _____

_____   _____   _____

Long, long ago

What kind of history does Haryana have, Daadu? Is it a very old state?

Well, Mishki. This region is where much of India's written history began. Come, let me tell you about it.

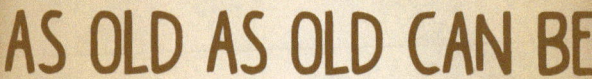

AS OLD AS OLD CAN BE

A lot of people believe that Haryana is where Hinduism was born. The Vedas, the ancient Hindu manuscripts, were also believed to have been written here. These were written when the Aryans made the north of India their home.

KURUKSHETRA—THE MIGHTIEST BATTLE OF ALL

The battle between the Kauravas and Pandavas is one of the greatest events in Hindu mythology. This great battle was fought at Kurukshetra in Haryana. It was during this battle that Lord Krishna had a divine discourse with Arjuna, the Pandava prince. This discourse came to be the Bhagwad Gita—the sacred book of the Hindus.

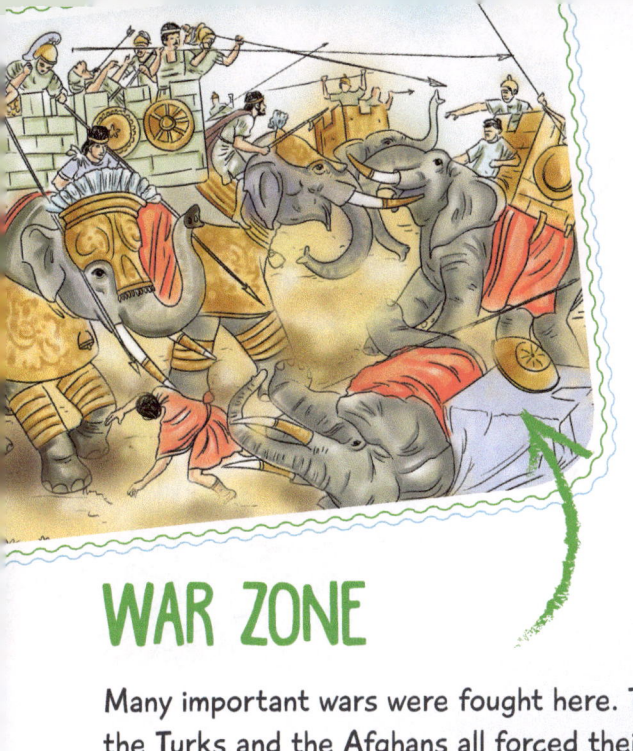

WAVES OF MIGRATION

Almost every invader who came into India from the north passed through Haryana. Alexander the Great too marched through this region, since Haryana lay in his path. He fought many battles here.

WAR ZONE

Many important wars were fought here. The Huns, the Turks and the Afghans all forced their way through this land, fighting battles as they went. Chandragupta Maurya overcame all the invaders and established the massive Mauryan Empire. During this period, Haryana and Punjab were considered one region.

Punjab, of which Haryana was a part, was called the Gateway to North India, because everyone entered India through it.

A bronze chariot commemorates the Battle of Kurukshetra.

MANY RULERS

The Huns, who were fierce warriors, forced their way into India from the north. They controlled the region for a while, but they were not effective rulers. They were defeated by a strong king called Harshavardhana, who went on to build a vast kingdom.

Harshavardhana was an amazing king. During his rule, education, culture and systems flourished. The famous Nalanda University was at its peak during his time.

THE DELHI SULTANATE

Harshavardhana finally became old and feeble, and his empire was soon dissolved. A few hundred years later, invaders like Muhammad of Ghazni and Muhammad Ghori started invading north India. A general called Qutb-ud-din Aibak laid the foundation of the Delhi Sultanate. The Lodhis were the last of the Delhi Sultanate to rule this area.

PANIPAT—HISTORY'S BATTLEGROUND

Panipat became the scene of some important battles that decided India's fate. Three major battles were fought here.

THE FIRST BATTLE OF PANIPAT

A powerful king named Babur established the Mughal Empire. He fought a fierce battle at Panipat against Ibrahim Lodhi, who was ruling the region as head of the Lodhi dynasty.

THE SECOND BATTLE OF PANIPAT

Babur's grandson Akbar the Great also fought a bloody war at Panipat—this time with a Hindu king named Hemu, who was trying to expand his kingdom. Akbar defeated him easily, and the Mughal rule continued—as strong as ever.

WOW! What a battle.

The Panipat battles inspired many artists to paint fearsome scenes of the battleground.

THE THIRD BATTLE OF PANIPAT

Years later, the Marathas were trying to advance into north India. A Muslim dynasty called the Durranis had defeated the Mughals and were in power in the region that is Haryana. There was a massive battle at Panipat between the Marathas and the Durranis, where the Durranis defeated the Marathas and held on tightly to their kingdom.

THE BRITISH ARRIVE

The British had long since identified India as a country they would like to rule. They had overcome other European powers like the Dutch and the Portuguese, and had taken over most of India. They easily overpowered the Mughals and what was left of the Durranis. They soon controlled all of India. During that time, Haryana was still a part of the Punjab state.

FIGHTING FOR INDEPENDENCE

The Indians united against the British. They did not want to be ruled by a foreign power. There were fights and revolts, and finally, in 1947, the British left and India became independent.

There were many confrontations between the British and the Indians, who fought each other fiercely.

TWO COUNTRIES

There were many arguments and disagreements in India between the Hindus and the Muslims. Each community wanted their own country. Finally, India was divided into India and Pakistan. Many Muslims would live in Pakistan and most Hindus would live in India. A part of the Punjab state went to Pakistan.

HARYANA IS BORN

WELCOME TO
HARYANA

All through this time, Haryana was still a part of Punjab, which consisted mainly of Punjabi-speaking Sikhs and Hindi-speaking Hindus. There was demand to split the state, which was supported by both communities. Finally, in 1966, Haryana became a separate state, made up mainly of Hindi-speaking people.

JUMBLED WORDS

Mishki is trying her best to remember all the history she has learnt. Help her unjumble the words so she remembers.

He fought Akbar in Panipat. _____ **MUEH**

Harshavardhana defeated this fierce warrior clan. _____ **UNSH**

They fought hard against the Durranis. _____ **SATHRAMA**

The mightiest battle of all time was fought here. _____ **ARTEHSKURUK**

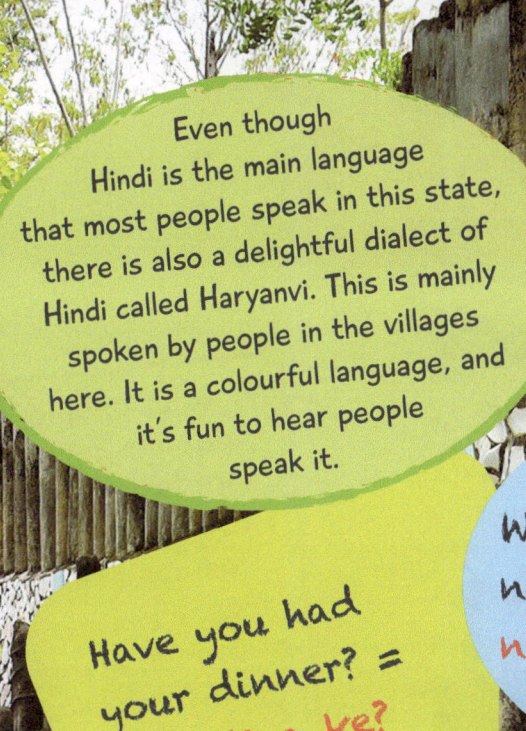

Even though Hindi is the main language that most people speak in this state, there is also a delightful dialect of Hindi called Haryanvi. This is mainly spoken by people in the villages here. It is a colourful language, and it's fun to hear people speak it.

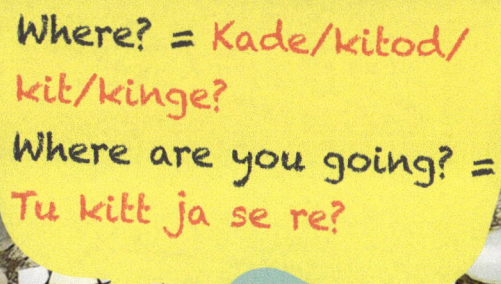

Where? = Kade/kitod/kit/kinge?
Where are you going? = Tu kitt ja se re?

Have you had your dinner? = Jeem liya ke?
Is all well? = Sab rajee khusee?

What is your name? = Kay naam se re tera?

What did you eat? = Tanne kay khaaya?

Come here = Urene aa
How are you? = Kay gyan se?

I don't know = Manne koni beraa

MATCH THE WORDS

Let's see how much you remember. Without looking at the words, match the English words to their Haryanvi translations.

Where are you going? | Have you had your dinner? | Come here | I don't know | How are you?

Kay gyan se? | Manne koni beraa | Tu kitt ja se re? | Jeem liya ke? | Urene aa

A peep into their life

Daadu, we have learnt about the history of Haryana. But how about the people who actually live here? What is their life like?

A lot of people who live here are farmers. They have many traditions and legends—and, of course, many festivals and dances too! They love having a good time.

A MIXED BAG

Hindus make up the largest number of people in this state. The Jats are the largest Hindu community and mainly comprise farmers. Many Muslims and Sikhs live here too. All these communities have their own festivals and culture. Come, let's explore some of these.

It's great to have cultural diversity.

GUGGA NAUMI

In Haryana, snakes are worshipped, because people believe that these slithering creatures will keep them safe from evil. During a festival called Gugga Naumi, people pray to a saint called Gugga Pir, who they believed had the power to cure people of dangerous snake bites.

GITA JAYANTI FESTIVAL

This festival is celebrated at Kurukshetra, the very place where Lord Krishna gave a discourse to Arjuna, which later became the Bhagwad Gita. During this week-long festival, there are recitals of holy scriptures from the Bhagwad Gita, bhajans (holy songs sung in praise of god) and dances that go on all night long.

Even I want to dance around that bonfire.

LOHRI

This popular festival, which is also celebrated in Punjab, marks the end of winter and the beginning of the harvest. People celebrate it by burning enormous bonfires. They dance around the fire in a circle, singing songs and throwing puffed rice into the fire.

23

SONG AND DANCE

SING A 'SAANG'

Saang (or *swaang* as it is sometimes called) is actually a form of mimicry. It is very popular in Haryana—as well as some of its neighbouring states. A group of ten to twelve people perform it. Sometimes, men dress as women and perform this. Through this performance, they enact religious stories or folktales.

KHORIA

This delightful dance is usually performed during weddings. The dancers wear bright skirts with billowing dupattas. One dancer begins by singing a folk song. The others join in and dance in a circle, twirling away. The women in the groom's family usually do this, while they wait for the groom to come back to his village with his new bride.

THE PHAG DANCE

This is also called the *phalgun* dance. It's very popular among the farming community during February and March, a time when farmers take a brief rest from their busy job. Men and women dress in their colourful best and celebrate the harvest.

LOOR

This fun dance is performed during Holi. Groups of girls sing in turn, clap and dance. The songs tell stories of falling in love, getting married and life after the wedding. It's a fun dance that is accompanied by a lot of laughter and joy.

DHAMAL DANCE

You could call this an emotional dance. People perform this to express love, joy, sorrow and hope. They say this dance style is so old that it was performed even during the times of the Mahabharata. The performers dance to the tune of the dholak, sarangi and *khartal*.

RHYME TIME

Pushka wants to find some words that rhyme with **DANCE** because he plans to write a poem. Follow the clues and help him find them.

_____ Jump around

_____ An opportunity

_____ A long spear

_____ In your own zone

PLAY ON

You can listen to this for hours!

HARYANAVI MUSIC

The folk music of Haryana is the foot-tapping kind and is very popular—not only in Haryana but in its neighbouring states too. There are some communities who are especially musical. Bhats, Jogis and Saangis are some of them. In fact, the musical tradition of this earthy state goes all the way back to Vedic times.

This state is probably the only one that has villages named after musical ragas. Ragas are musical compositions that were created by great musicians years and years ago.

MAKING MUSIC

Different clans and tribes play different musical instruments. Some of these are classical instruments that are difficult to master, but the folk musicians play them with ease. There are string instruments, like the sarangi; wind instruments, like the *been* (flute) and *shehnai*; and all sorts of bell and percussion instruments, like the dholak, *matka* and *damru*.

The people here are so creative that they even make music using matchsticks, papayas and the seeds of mangoes.

26

CROSSWORD TIME

Mishki wants to learn an instrument. But she must first learn to recognize them! Help her solve this picture crossword.

Bricks and stones

What kind of houses do people in Haryana live in, Daadu? You said there are many farmers here. But you also said there are lots of factories.

You are very sharp, Mishki. You're right. Because so much of Haryana is farmland, there are lots of rural houses. But in cities, there are modern flats and high-rise buildings too!

LOCAL IS BEST

In the villages of Haryana, farmers build homes using the local material. The houses are simple—made of mud, thatch and wood. And instead of expensive tiles, they simply coat the floor with dry cow dung mixed with mud. It might not sound appealing, but cow dung keeps the floor soft, clean and cool. Perfect for Haryana's hot summers!

COOKING IN THE OPEN

In the simple houses of Haryanvi villagers, cooking is a community affair, and kitchens are a simple open area, slightly separate from the rest of the house. On a mud stove, people cheerfully cook while they interact with the rest of the family.

HAVELI HO!

Wealthier people build large family homes called havelis. Large joint families live together in a haveli, which has many rooms. The haveli is decorated with traditional motifs. It almost always has a courtyard and elaborate gates. The courtyard is the centre of life—for family get-togethers, festivals or simply a place to sit around and chat.
Sounds cosy!

🏠 HOUSE HUNT

A haveli is a kind of a house. Can you circle the other words that are also the homes or houses in which people live?

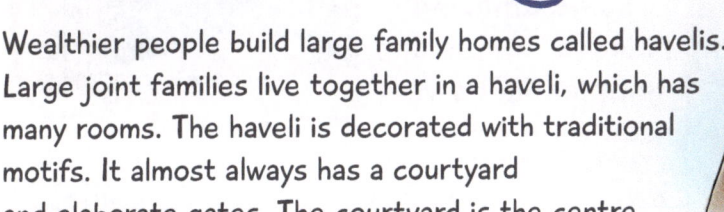

IGLOO GARAGE
WIGWAM COTTAGE
SKYSCRAPER
PARK CARAVAN
BUNGALOW CHIMNEY
GARDEN BEACH

I want to live in this haveli!

Standing strong

Now I am all ready to visit some monuments. There must be a lot to see in Haryana, Daadu.

Yes, indeed! Haryana was a very important place in Indian history, as we saw. And the kings that lived here built some amazing palaces, tombs and temples. Let's visit some right away.

PALACES AND TOMBS

The rulers of Haryana lived a royal life. They built beautiful palaces and tombs, many of which we can still see, though some are in ruins.

GUJARI MAHAL

A king called Firoz Shah Tughlaq built an entire palace for his beloved queen, Gujari Rani. There is a lovely story behind this. The king fell in love with Gujari while he was out hunting. She was a simple girl and was worried she might be mistreated by royal people, so she refused to go with him. He built this beautiful palace especially for her. That's what you call love!

FIROZ SHAH'S PALACE

The kings of those days sure knew how to live well. Firoz Shah Tughlaq built this palace hundreds of years ago for himself. One thing he took care of was making sure there was enough cover for his guards, to make sure no one attacked. There are secret passages, bastions, terraces and courtyards that help you imagine life in those ancient days.

What a pity that this palace is now in ruins!

JAL MAHAL

This lovely palace is built in the middle of a lake (actually a large tank). A man named Shah Quli Khan, who was Emperor Akbar's commander, built this pleasure palace. To enter the palace, you have to walk over a bridge.

Must have been a real pleasure to live in this palace.

BARSI GATE

Hansi is a walled city in Haryana. The Barsi Gate is one of the gates through which people enter this city. It is a lovely example of the architectural style of the Sultans who ruled at the time. There is an inscription in Persian on this gate that says that it was built by the famous Sultan Alauddin Khilji in 1303 CE. You feel royal marching through this gate, all right.

IBRAHIM LODHI'S TOMB

The brave king Ibrahim Lodhi, who was defeated by the Mughal emperor Babur in Panipat, lies buried in this tomb. The tomb is a simple affair, but it is an important historical landmark, for Lodhi's death was the event with which Mughal rule began.

CHOR GUMBAD

This one is interesting. This place, just like its name suggests, was at one point a hideout for burglars and thieves. It looks eerie and haunted. It was originally built as a tomb for a man called Jamaal Khan. Its isolated location made it perfect for thieves to hide in. People also call it *bhool bhulaiya* (a maze), because the passages are so complex, you could easily get lost in them.

This place can get scary on a dark night! So make sure you visit in broad daylight!

FAIRY TALE PALACE

Look at this enchanting palace. Can you find its exact shadow?

A

B

C

D

E

Help me out!

BU ALI SHAH'S TOMB

The tomb of a Muslim Saint called Bu Ali Shah Qualandar has an interesting Pied Piper—like story. People say that the town was infested with flies. Bu Ali Shah got rid of the flies for the people. But they still complained, and so, as punishment, he got the flies right back.

BIRBAL KA CHHATTA

This amazing palace was built during Emperor Shah Jahan's time. It is called Birbal ka Chhatta because Akbar and Birbal visited it. With lots of terraces, pavilions and fountains, it even had three underground floors—with natural light. Imagine that! Now it is in disrepair, but it must have been a busy place at one time.

A GRANDSON'S TRIBUTE

Ibrahim Khan Suri was an Afghan king who ruled over some parts of north India for a short period. He was killed during a battle and buried in Haryana. Many years after his death, his grandson built a beautiful tomb so that posterity could remember his grandfather.

A TOMB DEDICATED TO KHWAZA KHIZR

Khwaza Khizr was not an important historical figure, but his people must have loved him. He was a celebrity during his time. His tomb is a beautiful building made of red sandstone, with intricate patterns and a lovely gateway.

This is so beautiful!

A TOMB FOR HIMSELF

During the reign of Emperor Akbar, one of his commanders, Shah Quli Khan built a tomb for his father, but eventually he too was buried there. The tomb is an intricate structure that many people come to admire.

In those days, many rulers built their tombs well before they died, to make sure they were given the honour due to them.

WORD SEARCH

Can you help Pushka find four famous monuments hidden in the grid?

U	I	J	A	L	M	A	H	A	L	A
Y	O	P	L	K	J	H	G	F	D	S
G	U	J	A	R	I	M	A	H	A	L
T	R	E	W	Q	A	S	D	F	G	H
Q	C	H	O	R	G	U	M	B	A	D
A	M	N	B	V	C	X	Z	L	K	J
B	A	R	S	I	G	A	T	E	X	C

CHHACHHRAULI FORT

The raja of a place called Kalsia in Haryana built a magnificent fort for himself and his family. It had a palace with a throne room, magnificent murals on the walls, several reception rooms and many big courtyards. Now this lovely palace-fort has schools and offices inside it. Must be fun to study in a room where kings once lived!

PALACE OF MIRRORS

Royal people must have been vain in those days, because there are many *sheesh* mahals (palaces of mirrors) in India. The one in Haryana is beautiful. Today, there is a busy, bustling market all around it. It was built for the queen of a local king called Farrukh Shah. It has a stepwell, where the royal ladies would go to bathe. As the name suggests, there are lovely carved mirrors and many decorated arches that make the place a delight to see.

LOST

Mishki and Pushka are lost in this palace. Help them find their way out.

A MODERN WONDER

There was a small patch of land in Chandigarh (Haryana's capital) that was used as a garbage dump not so long ago. A Haryanavi man called Nek Chand saw this. He decided to use the garbage and make sculptures out of it. And so was born Chandigarh's famous Rock Garden.

DESIGN FROM WASTE

Nek Chand used all sorts of waste to create his sculptures. He used rusted mudguards from cars, old forks, cycle handlebars, torn tyres, broken marbles and even hair that he recovered from barber shops. As the number of sculptures increased, he began collecting discarded items from more and more places.

A KINGDOM OF DREAMS

When the government and other important people saw how beautiful these sculptures were, they supported Nek Chand. The garden was enhanced. He was given more land. And the whole place was made to resemble a palace with a royal garden. There are doorways, arches, courtyards and themed chambers; there are waterfalls, bridges and open-air theatres. And all of this was born from a dream of putting waste to use.

Crafty idea

Mishki and Pushka are so inspired by Nek Chand that they too want to make beautiful things from waste. They have decided to make pencil holders from toilet rolls. You can try it too.

You will need

- Three toilet roll tubes
- Coloured chart paper in your favourite colours
- Felt pens in your favourite colours
- Glue

Step 1 Cut discs using the chart paper.

Step 2 Stick the base of the roll on to the disc.

Step 3 Cut the coloured chart paper to fit around the toilet roll.

Step 4 Stick it right around the roll.

Step 5 Paint faces or patterns on the chart paper.

Your pencil holder is ready. Fill it with pencils, pens, brushes or scissors and keep it on your desk!

Working hard

Daadu, this seems like a state where people do many different things, because it has farmers as well as factories. What do most of the people actually do?

This is true. The people of Haryana have a lot of options to choose from. Many of them have been in their occupation for generations. Let's see what kind of work they do here.

Haryana has one of Asia's largest agriculture universities, where students go to learn new and modern farming technologies.

FARMER, FARMER, WHAT DO YOU GROW?

Farming is by far the most important occupation in Haryana. A lot of grains eaten in India are grown here. Farmers are busy all year round growing rice, wheat, sugarcane, corn, millet and a lot of other things. Cotton is also very important.

DAIRY DON

The farmers in Haryana also breed cows and buffaloes. In fact, Haryana is one of India's largest producers of milk and milk products. Some species of buffalo, like the Murrah water buffalo, are world-famous for their milk. There are thus many dairy farmers and milk societies where people work.

FACTORY FEVER

This amazing state is also one of India's most industrialized. Many international companies have their factories here. Cars, motorcycles, refrigerators, tractors and a whole lot of other things are made here. You can imagine how many people are employed in factories.

HANDY HANDICRAFTS

There are many thousands of villages in Haryana. For generations, villagers have developed skills in different areas, creating wonderful handicrafts that are now part of a thriving cottage industry. Let's see what Haryana's talented craftsmen make.

POTTERY MANIA

Pottery is an important occupation in this state. It's a family occupation, really. Potters work from their home. Usually, men give shape to the pots, and women decorate them with brilliant patterns and colours.

TERRIFIC TEXTILES

Some people call Panipat, the Textile Town. Traditional weavers who lived in Pakistan came and settled in Panipat after Independence. Haryana was one of India's largest cotton producers. This helped build the textile industry here. Many weavers innovated new techniques. Now, their textiles, like rugs and upholstery, are famous all over the world.

WEAVING FURNITURE

There are cloth weavers we all know about. But Haryana has many weavers who weave furniture. Amazing, isn't it? They weave stools called *moodhas*; they weave chairs of a reed called *sarkanda*; they marry the weave with wood and make small settees called *pidhis*.

This is so nice and comfortable.

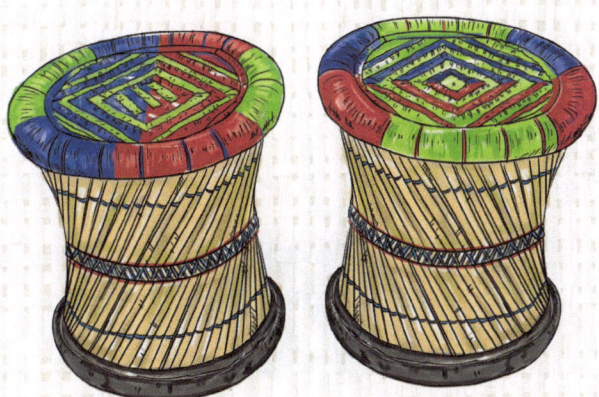

FIND THE WORD

There are six things that the people of Haryana are known for. Can you find all of them?

U	P	T	E	X	T	I	L	E	S
B	H	E	Y	Y	T	R	E	W	Q
H	A	N	D	I	C	R	A	F	T
B	F	A	C	T	O	R	I	E	S
Q	A	S	D	F	G	S	I	D	U
W	F	U	R	N	I	T	U	R	E
F	A	R	M	I	N	G	L	E	L
C	P	O	T	T	E	R	Y	K	G

Yum yum yum

I've been seeing people eat some interesting food. Daadu, my mouth is watering. Is it time to eat something and know about Haryana's food?

Haha, yes, Pushka. It's time. The food in Haryana is just like its people—interesting and earthy. Most of it is very healthy too! Come, let's discover some delicious dishes.

THE LAND OF ROTIS

The people of Haryana love their rotis— and are very innovative too. There are many kinds of rotis people eat. Bajra, jowar, wheat, barley and gram—each roti has its own unique taste. Sometimes stuffed with potato or sometimes by themselves, when these rotis are partnered with yummy veggie dishes, they taste like heaven.

MILKY WAY

The dairy produce of Haryana is famous. And the people here simply love their milk. They use milk to make yummy, thick lassi; they turn milk into thick butter that they liberally add dollops of on everything; they make loads of pure, rich ghee that they use to cook. But it is all healthy, so don't worry about having plenty of it.

CUCUMBER WITH A DIFFERENCE

Kachri is a kind of wild cucumber that is like a small melon. People make many kinds of dishes with kachri. They make chutneys, mix it with chillies or simply chop it up and make delicious dishes you can have along with rotis.

LAVISH LEFTOVERS

Ever thought that last night's rotis could taste so good? People in Haryana turn old rotis into a yummy dish called bhura-roti-ghee. Just like the name suggests, they mix stale rotis with ghee and powdered sugar (bhura).

HEALTHY TIMES

Feeling healthy? Then this dish called gajar-methi ki sabzi is perfect. It's a yummy mix of carrot and fenugreek.

SUPER SIDES
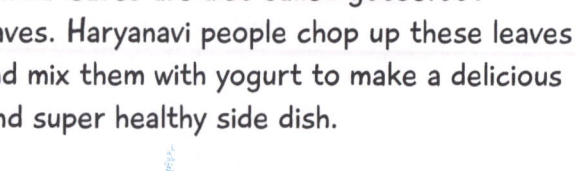

Bathua leaves are also called goosefoot leaves. Haryanavi people chop up these leaves and mix them with yogurt to make a delicious and super healthy side dish.

Yummmmy!!

HEALTHY LADDUS

People cook these little laddus called alsi ki pinni in Punjab as well. They are made of a seed called alsi and mixed with flour, ghee and sugar. The best thing about this sweet is that it is very healthy.

SWEET COMFORT

Mithe chawal is a sweet rice dish that's divinely comforting. It's a yummy mix of rice, sugar and ghee. You just can't say no to this dish.

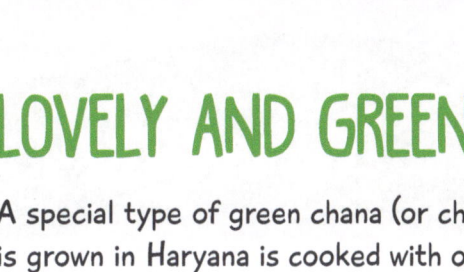

LOVELY AND GREEN

A special type of green chana (or chickpea) that is grown in Haryana is cooked with onion, tomato and lots of seasoning. It makes a great dish called hara dhania cholia that people eat with rotis.

A HEALTHY PORRIDGE

Bajre-ki-khichdi is a healthy porridge that is made with bajra (millet). It is a stand-alone meal that's ever so healthy. Don't forget the dollop of ghee. This healthy dish is much loved in other northern states too!

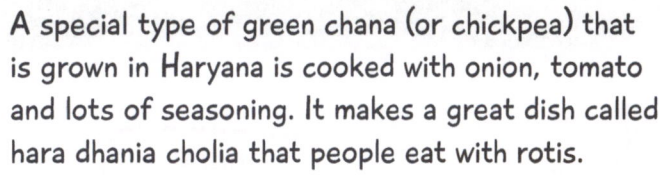

VEGETABLE SUDOKU

Pushka has decided to become healthy and is on a veggie diet. Help him solve this veggie sudoku. He must make sure that every row and column in each grid has at least one of the four vegetables.

 1
 2
 3
 4

What to wear?

Daadu, the people look very nice and colourful here. What kind of clothes do they traditionally wear?

You're right! The people, especially women in villages, wear colourful clothes. Now, people have modernized, but you will still find them wearing traditional attire in villages and during festivals.

COLOURFUL SPLENDOUR

Traditionally, women wore a long, colourful skirt that was called a *daaman*. They would team this with a long blouse called *kurti*. And a coloured cloth, often with gaily decorated patterns, would be used to cover the head and chest—just like a sari.

SIMPLE STYLE

The men have a very simple style of clothing. Typically, they wear a white dhoti, a white kurta and a long cloth on their shoulder. The colour in their clothing comes from the pagri (turban).

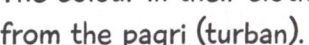

ALL DECKED UP

The women here love their chunky silver jewellery. From thick anklets to heavy neck pieces, waistbands and even head jewellery—the women often deck themselves up even on regular days. Always nice to be well turned out!

PAGRI PATTERNS

For men, the colour and the style in which they tie their pagri tell people a little about which community and region they belong to. It's not easy tying a pagri though. It's quite an art.

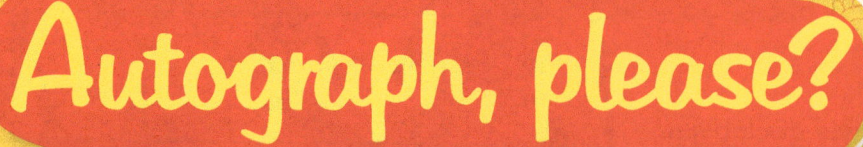
Autograph, please?

So, children, have you got your autograph books ready? Because even though this state is so small, it has produced some big names that have become famous.

Yes, we are ready. I love to meet famous people!

NEK CHAND

He was a simple man with a big vision. He had the idea of making a small garden in Chandigarh using old stones and recycled material. He worked at night, building his little garden. Soon, it began to attract visitors. Now, it attracts thousands of tourists every day and is a marvel to see.

Nek Chand has become world-famous for the incredible Rock Garden he built.

PANDIT JASRAJ

Born to a musical maestro, Pandit Jasraj is one of India's best known classical vocalists. He has performed all over the world, and his concerts are a joy for music lovers.

THE PHOGAT SISTERS

Mahavir Phogat, his daughters—Geeta, Babita, Ritu and Sangita—and his nieces—Priyanka and Vinesh—are all wrestlers. Mahavir Phogat beat the odds and trained them to become successful wrestlers.

The blockbuster movie *Dangal* was based on their lives.

SAKSHI MALIK

She is a gritty young wrestler who gave India its first medal in wrestling during the Asian Cup. She also won an Olympic bronze medal. She is an inspiration for young women in sport.

KALPANA CHAWLA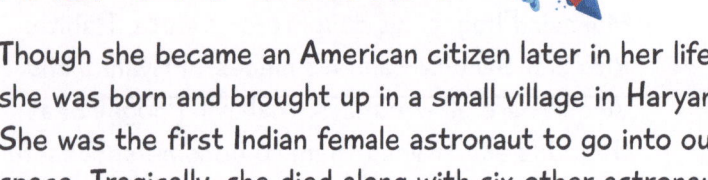

Though she became an American citizen later in her life, she was born and brought up in a small village in Haryana. She was the first Indian female astronaut to go into outer space. Tragically, she died along with six other astronauts, when one of their space missions went wrong.

KAPIL DEV

Kapil Dev Nikhanj is a cricketer, who was nicknamed the Haryana Hurricane. One of the most popular cricketing all-rounders of his time, he has captained India and played numerous matches in all formats.

VIJENDER SINGH

This young boxer gave India its first Olympic medal in boxing during the Beijing Summer Olympics. He was born and grew up in a small town in Haryana, where he got his first lessons in boxing.

SANTOSH YADAV

She is the first woman to climb Mount Everest not once but twice—and that too from the difficult side of Kangshung, a feat for even the most skilled mountaineer.

MATCH THEM RIGHT

Pushka is impressed with the people they have met. Can you match the name to the profession?

| Cricketer | Classical singer | Mountaineer | Wrestler |

| Santosh Yadav | Pandit Jasraj | Geeta Phogat | Kapil Dev |

Once upon a time . . .

Now for a nice story from Haryana. Daadu, there must be lots of folk tales from this lovely state. Can you tell us one?

THE JAT AND THE GIANT

Of course. Come and settle down. I will tell you the story of a Jat farmer and a giant.

One day, a Jat farmer named Harilal was returning to his village after selling his wares in the neighbouring village. His three sons accompanied him. The villages were far apart. Harilal was not a rich man. He didn't have a bullock cart to carry them all in comfort, so the entire family was walking.

The little group had walked many miles and was tired.

'Let us rest for a while below this tree,' Harilal said. They all sat in the shade of a large banyan tree. What they didn't know was that the banyan tree was the home of an ugly but gentle giant. The giant watched the family with interest.

Now, Harilal was a hardworking man. He couldn't bear to waste time. So he decided to make a rope while he rested.

'Go get some bamboo strands,' he told one son. Off the son went and got him some bamboo strands.

'Go get some water from the river,' he told his second son. Off the second went to get water.

'Light a fire so we can stay warm while we rest,' he told his third son, who obediently lit a fire. Soon, Harilal was busy making a rope while his sons rested.

The giant was watching all this. He became very curious, so he climbed down from his tree.

'What are you going to do with this rope?' he asked Harilal.

Harilal was startled seeing the giant—and a little scared too. But he decided not to show his fear.

'I am making this rope to tie you up with. Then, I will drown you in the river,' Harilal roared. What he didn't know was that the giant just looked scary but was quite a gentle soul.

'Oh, master,' the giant said, falling at his feet. 'Don't hurt me. I will give you a treasure chest if you leave me alone.'

Harilal was taken aback. His sons too awoke and watched in surprise. The giant clambered up the tree and soon came back with a huge treasure chest filled with gold coins.

'These are for you,' he said. 'You are a man to be obeyed. I saw how your sons obey you. Thank you for sparing me.' And saying that, the giant quickly disappeared up the tree.

Harilal and his sons lugged the precious treasure chest back with them to their village. They could not believe their luck.

Harilal became the richest man in his village.

When Ramprasad, his neighbour, heard about his good fortune, he wanted to try his luck too. But unlike Harilal, Ramprasad was a lazy, good-for-nothing fellow. He forced Harilal to tell him exactly what he had done and how he had got the chest of gold coins.

He took his three equally good-for-nothing sons along with him and went to the same banyan tree.

He settled under the tree and ordered his sons around just like Harilal had done.

'Fetch me some bamboo strands,' he ordered his first son.

'Get them yourself,' his son answered rudely and went off to sleep.

'Get me some water,' he ordered his second son.

'Get it yourself,' the second son retorted. And he turned around and was soon snoring.

'Light a fire,' he ordered his third son.

The third son did not even bother to reply. He simply found a comfortable spot and dozed off.

Ramprasad stood under the tree and yelled, calling out for the giant.

'You there! Come down. I want to tie you up,' he hollered.

The giant came down. He had a big smirk on his face.

'You want me to be afraid of you? Why, not even your sons are scared of you. Do what you want, I am off to sleep.' And saying so, the giant went back up the tree.

Poor Ramprasad was left staring. Not only did he not have the gold, he didn't have his sons' respect either.

TRAVEL DIARY

Have you enjoyed this trip to Haryana with your friends Mishki and Pushka—and, of course, with Daadu Dolma?

Now you can make your own Haryana diary. And if you ever visit Haryana, make sure you take pictures and put them in the photo box.

The first place I would visit in Haryana:

_____

If I were a farmer, I would grow:

_____

The one dish I am definitely going to eat:

_____

The monument I think is the most interesting:

_____

The one famous person from Haryana I would love to meet:

_____

I think the most interesting historical figure from Haryana was:

_____

The festival from Haryana that I think is the most fun:

_____

The five words that I think describe Haryana the best are:

_____

_____

_____

_____

_____

My Haryana memories:

ANSWERS

page 9 TREE PATTERN

 1   2   3

page 13 HIDDEN WORDS

Here are some of the words you can form: add, aid, air, bad, bid, dab, dad, fab, fad, far, fir, rib, rid, arid, bard, bird, fair, raid, braid, afraid

page 19 JUMBLED WORDS

HEMU, HUNS, MARATHAS, KURUKSHETRA

page 21 MATCH THE WORDS

Where are you going?— Tu kitt ja se r?; Have you had your dinner?— Jeem liya ke?; Come here—Urene aa; I don't know—Manne koni beraa; How are you?—Kay gyan se?

page 25 RHYME TIME

prance, lance, chance, trance

page 27 CROSSWORD TIME

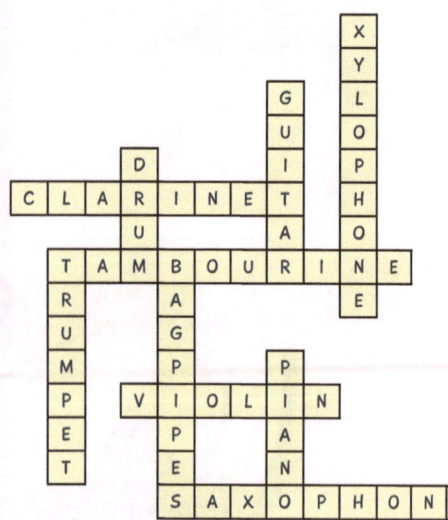

page 29 HOUSE HUNT

IGLOO, COTTAGE, SKYSCRAPER, CARAVAN, WIGWAM, BUNGALOW

page 33 FAIRY TALE PALACE

The exact shadow is E.

page 35 WORD SEARCH

U	I	J	A	L	M	A	H	A	L	A
Y	O	P	L	K	J	H	G	F	D	S
G	U	J	A	R	I	M	A	H	A	L
T	R	E	W	Q	A	S	D	F	G	H
Q	C	H	O	R	G	U	M	B	A	D
A	M	N	B	V	C	X	Z	L	K	J
B	A	R	S	I	G	A	T	E	X	C

page 37 LOST

page 43 FIND THE WORD

U	P	T	E	X	T	I	L	E	S
B	K	G	Y	Y	T	T	E	W	Q
H	A	N	D	I	C	R	A	F	T
B	F	A	C	T	O	R	I	E	S
Q	A	S	D	F	G	S	I	D	U
W	F	U	R	N	I	T	U	R	E
F	A	R	M	I	N	G	L	E	L
C	P	O	T	T	E	R	Y	K	G

page 43 VEGETABLE SUDOKU

(vegetable sudoku grid)

page 53 MATCH THEM RIGHT

Cricketer—Kapil Dev;
Classical singer—Pandit Jasraj;
Mountaineer—Santosh Yadav;
Wrestler—Geeta Phogat